Copyright © Gérald Vignaud Production
www.geraldvignaud.com
Version 1.0

Design: Elodie Su
Photo credit: Wolfgang Hasselmann

Edition: BoD - Books on Demand,
12/14 avenue des Champs-Élysées, 75008 Paris.
Printing: BoD - Books on Demand, Norderstedt, Germany

ISBN: 9782322273669
Legal deposit: February 2021

Gérald Vignaud

YOU GOT A PROBLEM ?

———

7 steps to effectively solve your biggest challenge

Foreword

I wrote this book as a continuation of my activities. It aims to share with you an effective methodology to solve your problems and thus bring your life into a new dimension. As you will discover, I ask many questions to which I invite you to reflect and answer in all sincerity. Also, regarding the use of this book, do not hesitate to break the rules and read it with a pen at hand. Write directly on it your answers to the questions in the proposed exercises. Write in the margins and on the blank pages all the ideas and thoughts that come to you. Highlight the passages and quotations that inspire you in fluorescent, dog-ear the pages and don't be afraid of damaging them. Never lose sight of the fact that a stoned book from which you have taken and integrated all the ideas is ten thousand times more valuable than a book that has never been opened and has been stored for years on a dusty shelf.

Also, please know that your feedback and ideas are essential to me. They help me to constantly question myself and to constantly improve what I have been doing for the past 20 years. In this age of the Internet and horizontal communication, reading a book without being able to communicate with its author seems to me to be, from my point of view, an inconsistency. So let's break this traditional pattern together and give us the possibility to contact each other if necessary.

I have the desire to meet virtually every reader of my book who wishes to do so. To do so, I have set up a free and private contact form on my site at the following address:

www.geraldvignaud.com/livre-contact

Do not hesitate to go there to share with me your results following the implementation of this problem solving process. I personally read all the messages and try to answer them as often as possible.

You can also find me on social networks:

As well as on my website:

www.geraldvignaud.com

See you soon,

Friendly,

Gérald Vignaud

Contents

If (You will be a man, my son!) 10

Introduction 13
The different types of problems

Chapter 1 23
Step 1: Understand that your problem is a gift!

Chapter 2 33
Step 2: Adopt the right physiognomy and state of mind for its resolution

Chapter 3 41
Step 3: Analyze the situation from an external, positive, emotionally detached and global point of view

Chapter 4 49
Step 4: Begin conceptualizing your problem-solving process

Chapter 5 67
Step 5: Take massive action!

Chapter 6 75
Step 6: Identify the results you have achieved and continually adjust your approach until you get the results you are looking for

Chapter 7 85
Step 7: Welcome your successes but also accept what cannot be changed by using the emotion generated as a leverage for your life

It was simply inconceivable for me to write a book like this one without evoking this magnificent poem by Rudyard Kipling. He wrote it in 1910, for his then 13-year-old son.

Published under the English title "If", this text is, in my opinion, one of the most beautiful and powerful poems ever written. And since it has now fallen into the public domain, it is therefore with great pleasure that I share it here, as a preamble to this work, to invite you to (re)discover it. ☺

If (You will be a man, my son!)

If you can keep your head when all about you
   Are losing theirs and blaming it on you,
If you can trust yourself when all men doubt you,
   But make allowance for their doubting too;
If you can wait and not be tired by waiting,
   Or being lied about, don't deal in lies,
Or being hated, don't give way to hating,
   And yet don't look too good, nor talk too wise:

If you can dream—and not make dreams your master;
   If you can think—and not make thoughts your aim;
If you can meet with Triumph and Disaster
   And treat those two impostors just the same;
If you can bear to hear the truth you've spoken
   Twisted by knaves to make a trap for fools,
Or watch the things you gave your life to, broken,
   And stoop and build 'em up with worn-out tools:

If you can make one heap of all your winnings
   And risk it on one turn of pitch-and-toss,
And lose, and start again at your beginnings
   And never breathe a word about your loss;
If you can force your heart and nerve and sinew
   To serve your turn long after they are gone,
And so hold on when there is nothing in you
   Except the Will which says to them: 'Hold on!'

If you can talk with crowds and keep your virtue,
   Or walk with Kings—nor lose the common touch,
If neither foes nor loving friends can hurt you,
   If all men count with you, but none too much;
If you can fill the unforgiving minute
   With sixty seconds' worth of distance run,
Yours is the Earth and everything that's in it,

  And -which is more- you'll be a man, my son!

Rudyard Kipling (1865-1936)

Introduction

The different types of problems

> "Each problem has hidden in it an opportunity so powerful that it literally dwarfs the problem. The greatest success stories were created by people who recognized a problem and turned it into an opportunity."
>
> *Joseph Sugarman*

As she is beset by her daily problems, a young woman comes to seek refuge with her parents in the hope of finding comfort there. As soon as she arrives, she collapses with tears in her eyes in her mother's arms. She sobbed and explained to her that she could no longer bear her life full of problems that she was tired of dealing with all the time. As soon as she settles one problem, a new one that is even more complicated appears... She is fed up and wants to drop everything.

Without saying anything, his mother takes his hand and brings her into the kitchen. She takes three pots, fills them with water and places them on the hot plates which she turns on. Once the water starts to boil, she places carrots in the first pot. In the second one an egg and in the third one a few spoons of ground coffee. Still without saying anything, she lets it boil. 15 minutes later, she takes out the carrots and puts them on a plate, the egg in a bowl and the coffee in a cup.

    - What do you see? she asks her daughter.

    - Carrots, an egg and coffee! she replies.

The mother asks her to come closer and touch the carrots, which have all become soft. She then asks her to take the hardened egg and break its shell. Finally she holds out the cup and asks her to taste the coffee.

- What are you trying to tell me, Mum? she asks her.

- Look at my daughter, each of these three elements faced the same boiling water, but each of them reacted differently. The carrot went in hard and strong but came out soft and weak. The egg, on the other hand, was all liquid inside, but the test of boiling water made it all hard. And the ground coffee turned the boiling water into a very pleasant drink.

She then looks at her child with a deep and loving gaze.

- My daughter, she said, how do you react in the face of adversity? Are you a carrot that seems strong on the surface, but when faced with problems you become soft? Are you an egg that becomes hardened by the problems it faces? Or are you that coffee that turns problem into opportunity?

There is something in life that affects absolutely everyone: the problems we encounter. And, apart from the stories of bathtubs leaking and filling up at the same time as the fifth-grade teacher suggests, it is unfortunately not at school that we learn this fundamental element of any life: how to effectively solve a problem. It is on this subject that I would like to speak to you here.

But first of all, you need to understand what a problem really is, what the different types of problems are and what impact they can have on your life.

It's a fact: almost generally speaking, people don't like to get into trouble. But the interesting thing, if we take the analysis a little further, is that the only people who don't have problems are in a cemetery. In fact, what I mean by this is that as long as you're alive, it's mathematical: you're unstoppably experiencing problems.

The aim is then not only to know how to solve them but to determine their origins in order to act accordingly to ensure that they are not renewed.

There are three types of problems:

- Common and normal problems: Common and normal problems are those that happen regularly and that you deal with easily. They come into your life, you analyze them, solve them, learn from them and forget them. Expect to face these types of problems very regularly because they are inseparable from life and allow you to make it evolve.

- Abnormal problems: Abnormal problems are those that you think you have solved but which, structurally, are still present in you. In other words, you have solved the consequence (the problem) but not the source (the very structure of your functioning or your environment that created the problem), which makes these problems keep reappearing in your life in a new form. Abnormal problems are toxic because they can lock you into a certain stage of your life and block its development.

- Pathological problems: Pathological problems are chronic abnormal problems which, again, come back again and again but which can have extremely serious consequences on your life. If these problems are not detected and treated, they can have very serious consequences. Pathological problems can turn your life into a complete physical, emotional and financial failure. They can even threaten your very survival.

Whatever category they belong to, and in order to help you solve them, I have conceptualized a problem-solving process especially for you. It consists of seven steps.

- Step 1: Understand that your problem is a gift!

- Step 2: Adopt the right physiognomy and state of mind for its resolution

- Step 3: Analyze the situation from an external, positive, emotionally detached and global point of view

- Step 4: Begin conceptualizing your problem-solving process

- Step 5: Take massive action!

- Step 6: Identify the results you have achieved and continually adjust your approach until you get the results you are looking for

- Step 7: Welcome your successes but also accept what cannot be changed by using the emotion generated as a leverage for your life

Now, is this problem solving process perfect? No. Does it work 100% on all types of problems? Probably not.

On the other hand, I guarantee two things: on the one hand, it will enable you to solve most of them and, on the other hand, it will bring you a new and constructive approach to each of your most complex and/or insoluble problems. And in order to validate its effectiveness, I propose today to test this resolution process <u>on your biggest current problem</u>. To begin, ask yourself the right questions and take the time to answer them in writing:

What exactly is my biggest problem right now? How would I define it?

_____
_____
_____
_____
_____
_____
_____

What are the different factors in my problem? What are the source, nature, causes, challenges, unknowns, issues and consequences?

_____
_____
_____
_____
_____
_____
_____

Why is this a problem?

___

What kind of problem is it? Is it normal, abnormal or pathological? Why?

___

What emotional state does this problem put me in? Why does it put me in this state?

_____
_____
_____
_____
_____
_____
_____
_____
_____
_____

Is this emotional state conducive to solving my problem or not? Why or why not?

_____
_____
_____
_____
_____
_____
_____
_____
_____
_____

What would be the different possible developments for me to consider my problem solved?

_____
_____
_____
_____
_____
_____
_____
_____
_____
_____
_____
_____
_____
_____
_____
_____

"A problem well-defined is a problem half solved."

John Dewey

Chapter 1

Step 1: Understand that your problem is a gift!

Step 1: Understand that your problem is a gift!

"Understanding that your problem is a gift!" is the first step in our problem solving process.

Let me explain: by answering the questions above, you have identified what your biggest problem is. Top. But now I'm going to tell you the truth, and it's up to you to hear it:

You think that's your biggest problem? It's not! I'll tell you: your biggest problem is not this problem, your biggest problem is that you think it's a problem!

Problems are a gift and you must use them to take your life to the next level. Because in order to grow and move forward in life, you need opponents: that's part of it! Without adversaries, without opponents, there can be no personal growth. If you reach your goals without struggling, not only is it no fun, but you don't learn!

And the pattern is always the same: the process of getting through a problem always breaks down into seven elements. Seven components that follow a precise chronology.

      1/ Desire
      2/ The problem
      3/ The opponent
      4/ The plan
      5/ The fight
      6/ Self-revelation
      7/ The new balance

1/ Desire: In the beginning, you are there, in your life, in balance. Everything is stable and, consciously or not, you desire more.

2/ <u>The problem:</u> And there, at some point, in one form or another, a problem arises.

3/ <u>The opponent:</u> And with this problem comes -always- an opponent. An opponent who can take three different forms:

- An **external** opponent: This is a person you don't know, outside your life, who hits it more or less violently.

- An **internal** opponent: This is someone close to you who you know well -even very, very well- and who opposes you.

- An **intimate** opponent: This is one of your ghosts, a poorly programmed part of yourself that acts against your interests. This intimate adversary can take many forms: a buried and uncontrolled fear that comes back, a lack of strength or courage, or that other part of you that comes out, regains control and sabotages everything...

4/ <u>The plan:</u> After the first few moments when you can't do anything else but realize the situation and try to absorb the shock as best you can, it's time to react by drawing up a plan to counter this opponent.

5/ <u>The fight:</u> The fight will be the implementation of the plan drawn up. But the theory will be mixed with the reality on the ground and, inevitably, unexpected things will happen and make the situation more complex. Sometimes it will be even worse because absolutely nothing will happen as planned. A moment of loss of hope and a desire to give up everything usually occurs at this point. A completely normal sequence, one or more moments of discouragement being most often part of the classic course of a fight.

6/ <u>Self-revelation:</u> Then comes the moment of the click, the moment when you get your act together and the wheel turns (in this order or in the opposite order, the Universe never lets us down). You then regain control of the situation and reach the next level, the level that allows you to triumph over your opponent, whether external, internal or intimate…

A self-revelation is a trigger that transforms your way of thinking and acting and whose consequences can take many forms: new beliefs, new values, new skills or new character traits such as a deeper level of determination, courage, faith, honesty, etc.

7/ <u>The new balance:</u> Having triumphed over the situation, your life is back in balance, as before, but with one notable difference: you have enlarged your comfort zone. A comfort zone whose enlargement is proportional to the difficulty of the fight you have just fought. And you will live in this new balance until a new problem arises and a new cycle of these seven elements begins. And so on and so forth…

And even if there may be some variations, this is the pattern for all true stories, large or small. Whether they are past, present or future.

This seven-element scheme is so universal that it is used in all successful film scripts. Let's take the film Star Wars as an example, and let's take a look at it:

- <u>Element 1 - Desire:</u> At the beginning of the film, Luke Skywalker is in element 1 of the cycle, that of desire. His life is in balance: he is a farmer at his uncle's farm but he dreams of more and wants to become a pilot for the Rebel Alliance. But his uncle puts the brakes on him and gives him the pretext of the coming harvests to stay on the farm with him.

- Element 2 - The Problem: It is through the two droids carrying Leila's message for Obi-Wan Kenobi that the problem arrives for Luke. The Empire, which pursues the Droids, exterminates his family and pushes him to leave to face Obi-Wan Kenobi, his new opponent (the Empire).

- Element 3 - The opponent: In Star Wars, the first opus of the Saga, Luke's opponent is external: The Empire represented by the Death Star and Darth Vader.

    A *small parenthesis:* it is interesting to see the evolution of Luke's opponent during the first trilogy. External (the Empire, represented by the Death Star and Darth Vader) in Star Wars, his opponent also becomes internal when, in Empire Strikes Back, he learns his relationship with Darth Vader. He then becomes intimate when, in "The Return of the Jedi", he leads this fight against himself in order not to fall into the dark side of the Force.

- Element 4 - The plan: Together with the rebels, he elaborates the plan to fight and destroy his opponent, the main weapon of the Empire: The Death Star.

- Element 5 - Fighting: The fight is on. All ships of the Rebel Alliance attack the Death Star. But nothing happens as planned: they miss their target and the Empire retaliates by sending fighters to counter-attack.

    We are close to the end: all the rebel ships supposed to destroy the Death Star are being shot down one after the other by the Empire's fighters and the Death Star is preparing to fire on the rebel base, which will result in the final extermination of all its members. Darth Vader himself flies a fighter that methodically pursues and destroys one by one the last rebel X-wings. Luke's ship being the last one still in place, he becomes de facto the last hope. A slim hope who is close to being shot by a clever and determined Darth Vader...

- <u>Element 6 - Self-disclosure:</u> Luke has a tiny and unique chance to launch his missile and destroy the Death Star. That's when self-disclosure happens! Or rather a double self-revelation: The one by Han Solo who initially decided to leave with the money and who finally changed his mind to come back and help Luke in the battle, a crucial help. And of course, that of Luke himself who, against all odds, unplugged his onboard computer and decided to trust the Force. During this decisive moment, he remains ultra-concentrated, fires his missile at the right moment and destroys the Death Star!

- <u>Element 7 - The new balance:</u> Following his victory, Luke finds a new balance where he blossoms at a higher level. And as a symbol of this new balance, the final battle scene ends with a message he receives in a dream-vision from his mentor Obi-Wan Kenobi: *"Remember Luke, Force will be with you. Always!"*

A new balance that will of course be upset in the following films. New problems will emerge and new opponents will join in, thus creating an <u>endless cycle of these seven elements</u> that will make Luke grow more and more during his epic...

And whether in fiction or in real life, it's always the same: the main ingredient of the story is the hero's weakness. This is the main source of the whole adventure, to see how the central character - that is you- will solve this character flaw he has at the beginning of the story.

The morality of it all? To grow up, you have to have a problem! And I'll go even further and say that the quality of your life is in direct proportion to your ability to live with insecurity, your ability to cope with problems. Whatever you think about it, your biggest problem today, whatever it is, has one or more hidden gifts and you have to see it as such.

Again, ask yourself the right questions: What is positive about my current problem and its consequences? What are the hidden gifts? Why? Take the time to think about it and write down all your answers.

_____
_____
_____
_____
_____
_____
_____
_____
_____
_____
_____
_____
_____
_____
_____

"Behind every problem is a gift
that you have to know how to appreciate."

Steve Lambert

Chapter 2

Step 2: Adopt the right physiognomy and state of mind for its resolution

Step 2: Adopt the right physiognomy and state of mind for its resolution

I have a very powerful personal belief. A belief that gives me power and that I invite you to integrate: in life, there are no victims, there are only volunteers!

By this I mean that even if you are not always responsible for the events that happen -even if, in spite of everything, directly or indirectly, this is very often the case- you are completely in control, and therefore responsible, for the reaction that you decide to have towards them.

And since problems are a gift, I suggest you decide to use them to take your life to another level.

But first of all, you will have to regain control of your physiognomy and your state of mind. There are three things you need to do to do this:

- Your focus

    o Your focus is where you direct your thoughts and therefore your actions. It's just like driving a car: it goes where you look. So, to get you in the right direction, decide to focus your thoughts in the right direction!

- Your communication with yourself

    o When a situation arises in front of you, a question like "What is positive about this situation?" will give you a lot more power than a shitty question like "Why does it always fall on me?". So, choose wisely the questions you ask yourself.

- Each word has a definition and an emotional charge -positive or negative- of its own. Emotion being the leverage that multiplies you or, conversely, deprives you of your power, decides to use a transformational vocabulary. For example:
    - Replace the word "problem" with a more appropriate word, such as "challenge", "circumstance" or "situation".
- Replace phrases that depress you with phrases that empower you and allow you to take action! Here's a concrete example:
    - I'm poor > It's a depressing phrase that diminishes your power.
    - I'm mowed > It's better because it's more neutral and temporal.
    - I have 50 cents left in my account > Facts presented in this way only offer you possibilities for development. ☺

- Your physiognomy
    - If your mind influences your body, know that the reverse is also true! Consequently, decide to control your physiognomy:
        - Straighten your shoulders and stand up straight.

- Raise your gaze upwards.
- Breathe deeply, through the lower abdomen.
- Smile to life and to the world!

Getting back in control of your focus, your internal communication and your physiognomy will put you back in control of your life and give you the keys to dominate your problem.

Once you have regained control of yourself, you will then have to create a sufficiently powerful emotional leverage. A force that will come from inside you and that will push and motivate you. This force will be your "why", the "why" of your problem must absolutely be solved. Your "Why" has to be emotionally very strongly charged. <u>It has to take you by the guts and obsess you day and night</u>, literally.

To do this, start by thinking about the fundamental and emotionally charged reason why your problem <u>needs to </u>be solved.

Think about the directions your life will take if you solve this challenge. What will be the consequences and positive impacts on it. Imagine what new possibilities will open up for you. Visualize and feel the positive emotions you will experience if you succeed.

And conversely, ask yourself what will become of your life and what the negative impacts will be if you don't manage to solve your problem. What are the problems that will happen to you? What ordeals are you going to go through? What levels of anxiety and pain will you experience? Visualize and feel all the pain and negative emotions that you will go through if you fail.

Whether positive or negative, don't hesitate to amplify all these emotions and sensations to the maximum in order to anchor them powerfully in you. The science of Neuro Linguistic Programming (NLP) explains that in an unconscious way, the human being acts permanently to move closer to pleasure and away from pain (it should be noted, by the way, that it will take much more energy to move away from pain than to move closer to pleasure). It is therefore a question here of programming your nervous system by integrating your "Why" in order to condition you to move towards it. This is why it is so important that it has a very strong emotional charge.

Understand that if you develop a powerful enough "Why", then you will have no difficulty in finding and implementing a "How" that will come to you on its own.

What is my "Why", that fundamental and emotionally charged reason why I have to solve this problem? Why is it so important to me?

_____
_____
_____
_____
_____
_____
_____
_____
_____
_____

What directions will my life take if I solve this challenge? What will be the consequences and positive impacts on it? What new possibilities will open up for me? What positive emotions will I feel? What are the reasons for this?

_____
_____
_____
_____
_____
_____
_____
_____
_____
_____
_____
_____
_____
_____
_____
_____
_____
_____
_____
_____
_____
_____
_____

Conversely, what will become of my life and what will be the negative impacts if I don't manage to resolve it? What are the problems that will happen to me? What calvaries will I go through? What levels of anguish and pain will I experience?

_____
_____
_____
_____
_____
_____
_____
_____
_____
_____
_____
_____
_____

"The state of mind is three-quarters of what counts. So, you have to maintain it carefully if you want to do something big and lasting."

Paul Gauguin

_____

Chapter 3

Step 3: Analyze the situation from an external, positive, emotionally detached and global point of view

Step 3: Analyze the situation from an external, positive, emotionally detached and global point of view

That's it, you know that your problem is a gift, you have put yourself in the right state of mind, physical and emotional to solve it and you have a powerful "Why" as a driving force. Now you will have to analyze it in order to redirect it towards its solution. And for your analysis to be effective, you will need to step back from the situation to see it from an external, positive, detached and global point of view.

Dissociate yourself emotionally from your problem in order to take a neutral view of it and above all make a distinction: do not confuse a problem that, once solved, will be forgotten and buried forever (which is the case for most of them) with a more complex or even insoluble situation, the consequences of which will still be visible in years or even decades to come.

Analyzing your problem to redirect it towards its solution will be done in 3 phases:

Phase 1: Be objective with yourself and see things as they really are, without letting your emotions artificially make them worse.

- Awaken your mind to the reality of the situation. See the facts objectively and as they really are, without the filter of your emotions and your programming or mind conditioning.
- Really identify your problem. Clearly define why it is a problem by putting specific words to it. Then ask yourself objectively: Is this really my problem or is it just the cover-up of something else? And if so, what is that something else?

Phase 2: Also identify the positive things that this situation brings to you. And there are always positive things! Here are a few examples:

- If your problem is that your partner, who is also your best friend, has swindled and robbed you, the good news is that you have finally opened your eyes to who he really is.
- If your problem is that your wife has just left you for another man, the positive is that this can lead you to question yourself and to identify, analyze and correct certain behaviours.
- If your problem is that you've just been diagnosed with cancer, the good news is that at least now you know exactly what you have. This allows you to move on to the "fight" phase, the one before recovery.

Generally speaking, every problem we encounter forces us to go outside our comfort zone, bringing new awareness, new things learned, new people met, new decisions made, etc. etc. Each of these elements is potentially the bearer of positive things, it's up to you to know how to detect them.

Phase 3: No matter what difficulties you face in the moment, look at things in a better light by creating a positive vision of how they might happen in the future.

- Those who solve problems effectively see what no one else sees and benefit from it. They conceive a vision of what could be, an irresistible future and begin to anticipate it. Don't forget that often a clearly stated problem is already half solved.

IMPORTANT: Confusion means you don't understand, you don't know. Confusion is the first step in the solution. If you're confused, you're close to a click. So, welcome this confusion with kindness!

I objectively list all the aspects and data of my challenge. I see things as they really are, not worse than they are.

_____
_____
_____
_____
_____
_____
_____
_____
_____
_____
_____
_____
_____
_____
_____
_____
_____
_____
_____
_____
_____
_____

I really identify my problem and clearly define why it is one by putting precise words on it.

_____
_____
_____
_____
_____
_____
_____
_____
_____

I ask myself objectively: Is this really my problem or is it hiding something else? And if so, what exactly?

_____
_____
_____
_____
_____
_____
_____
_____
_____

What positive things does this situation bring me despite all this?

How could I see things in a better light? What positive and constructive developments could take place in this situation?

_____
_____
_____
_____
_____
_____
_____
_____
_____
_____
_____
_____
_____
_____
_____
_____
_____
_____
_____
_____

"When you can't go back, you have to worry only about the best way of moving forward."

Paulo Coelho

Chapter 4

Step 4: Begin conceptualizing your problem-solving process

Step 4: Begin conceptualizing your problem-solving process

In the previous step, you created a positive and constructive vision of how things might happen in the future. Now it's time to start conceptualizing your problem-solving process to create things according to your vision. To do this, the direction of your focus is crucial. You need to spend only 5% of your time on the problem and 95% on the solution. <u>A solution that spends most of its time optimizing its resources.</u>

First, start by asking yourself the right questions:

- Has anyone anywhere on Earth, in the past, ever successfully experimented and solved this same problem? (On the Internet is most likely this information, you just have to go and look for it.) Who is it?

- If so (which is most of the time the case), how did he do it? (Again, an Internet search will most likely give you this information.)

- How to identify and model a part or even the whole solution?

Afterwards, make a list of the people -physical and moral- who could, in one form or another, provide you with possible help. This list will obviously vary according to the problem you have to deal with. Here are a few examples:

- Your family and friends with whom you could talk about your problem so that they can share an external analysis of the situation with you.
- People who would like to help you solve it

- People who are directly affected by your problem and who have an interest in solving your problem.
- People who have resources that could help you solve it
- People who know people who could help you
- Professionals who could bring you their expertise and/or competence (e.g. doctor, lawyer, craftsman, plumber, coach, therapist, etc.).
- Companies that could bring you their products or services (e.g. transport company, software publisher, laboratory, etc.).
- Public institutions and administrations (e.g. police, hospital, tax department, etc.)

Sometimes we solve our problems alone, but often external help is indispensable. It is not impossible that you may need the help of some of the people on this list to solve your challenge. You can of course put on this list people that you know little or not yet but that you will contact if necessary. A list that you will obviously make grow as you think about it.

Then, invent and visualize all possible ways to solve this situation. Brainstorm -alone or with one or more of the people on your list- and make up an inventory of all the potential solutions -even the most stupid, impractical and far-fetched ones- that you can think of. At first, write down all your raw ideas without any censorship, you will sort them out afterwards, and only afterwards. This is very important, because <u>by really evaluating all ideas without any filter, you can either finally find that a seemingly crazy idea is not so crazy,</u> or you can take the basis of an unfeasible solution and make it evolve into something more efficient which will eventually become the solution you are looking for.

And now, once your list of solution ideas has been pushed to the limit, you sort it out: among all these solution ideas, which ones can be seriously considered?

Among all these potential ideas, select the ones you think are the best three.

Then, faced with these three potential solutions, review the resources you already have and those you need.

Ask yourself:

- To apply this solution to my problem, what resources do I need?

- Which ones do I already have?

- Which ones can I possibly have?

- Which ones do I miss? How can I acquire them?

Resources that can be intimate, internal and/or external and that can take different forms. For example:

- a new way of seeing things and/or functioning
- more energy
- more personal serenity
- time
- money
- talent
- one (or more) piece(s) of information

- knowledge
- skills
- attentive listening
- a capacity for analysis
- human resources, connections

Important: All great leaders know that resources are never a problem because there is always a way to acquire them. Therefore, more than money, time or skills, the ultimate resources are human emotions, including envy, creativity, certainty, determination, determination, flexibility, passion, compassion and vision.

Identifies the advantages and disadvantages of each of the three solutions.

Finally, with this new visibility, decide which of these three solutions you will choose, the one you consider the most suitable for the resolution of your challenge.

Is there anyone anywhere in the past who has successfully experienced and solved the same situation I am experiencing today? (The answer to this question is most likely to be found on the Internet, you just have to go and look for it.) Who is it?

_____
_____
_____
_____

If so (which is most of the time the case), how did he do it? (Again, an Internet search will most likely give you this information.)

_____
_____
_____
_____
_____
_____
_____
_____
_____
_____
_____
_____

How can I model a part or even the entire solution?

_____
_____
_____
_____
_____
_____
_____
_____
_____
_____
_____
_____
_____

I make a list of all the people who could, in one form or another, help me in some way:

_____
_____
_____
_____
_____
_____
_____
_____
_____
_____
_____
_____
_____
_____
_____
_____
_____
_____
_____
_____
_____
_____
_____
_____

I invent and visualize all the possible ways to solve this situation: I brainstorm -alone or with one or more of the people on my list- and I make an inventory of all the potential solutions, even the most stupid and impractical ones. For the moment, I put all my ideas in the raw and without any censorship, I will sort them out afterwards.

_____
_____
_____
_____
_____
_____
_____
_____
_____
_____
_____
_____
_____
_____
_____
_____
_____
_____
_____
_____
_____
_____
_____

Now is the time to sort out: among all these ideas for solutions, which ones can be seriously considered? Which ones can be seriously considered?

_____
_____
_____
_____
_____
_____
_____
_____
_____
_____
_____
_____
_____

I select the three most possible solutions:

_____
_____
_____

For each of the three potential solutions, review the resources you already have and those you need. Ask yourself:

- *Potential solution number **1**:*

To apply this solution to my problem, what resources do I need?
_____
_____
_____
_____
_____
_____

Which ones do I already have?
_____
_____
_____
_____
_____

Which ones can I possibly have?
_____
_____
_____
_____
_____
_____

Which ones do I miss? How can I acquire them?

_____
_____
_____
_____
_____
_____

What are the **advantages** if I choose to apply this solution? What are the benefits?

_____
_____
_____
_____
_____
_____

What are the **disadvantages** if I choose to apply this solution? What are the disadvantages?

_____
_____
_____
_____
_____
_____

- <u>*Potential solution number **2**:*</u>

To apply this solution to my problem, what resources do I need?
_____
_____
_____
_____
_____
_____
_____

Which ones do I already have?
_____
_____
_____
_____
_____
_____

Which ones can I possibly have?
_____
_____
_____
_____
_____
_____

Which ones do I miss? How can I acquire them?

_____
_____
_____
_____
_____
_____

What are the **advantages** if I choose to apply this solution? What are the benefits?

_____
_____
_____
_____
_____
_____

What are the **disadvantages** if I choose to apply this solution? What are the disadvantages?

_____
_____
_____
_____
_____
_____

- *Potential solution number 3:*

To apply this solution to my problem, what resources do I need?
_____
_____
_____
_____
_____
_____
_____

Which ones do I already have?
_____
_____
_____
_____
_____
_____

Which ones can I possibly have?
_____
_____
_____
_____
_____
_____
_____

Which ones do I miss? How can I acquire them?

_____
_____
_____
_____
_____

What are the **advantages** if I choose to apply this solution? What are the benefits?

_____
_____
_____
_____
_____

What are the **disadvantages** if I choose to apply this solution? What are the disadvantages?

_____
_____
_____
_____
_____

And now, according to all these elements, what is the priority solution I choose, the one I consider the most suitable? Why is that?

_____
_____
_____
_____
_____
_____
_____
_____
_____
_____
_____
_____
_____
_____
_____
_____
_____

"There is no human problem that cannot be solved because the solution is within us."

Alfred Sauvy

Chapter 5

Step 5: Take massive action!

Step 5: Take massive action!

If you have followed the process correctly, you now have a better view of the situation, the resources available to you, the potential solutions that exist and you have decided which one you are going to use to solve your problem. Now, if you want results, you have to provoke them and you will have to take <u>massive action</u>. Here are the five phases for effective action:

<u>1/ Lists all the actions to be considered.</u>

- Which are the most important?

- Which are the most urgent?

- Which ones are essential? Why are they necessary?

<u>2/ Assess whether there is a particular timing or agenda</u> that you need to take into account in order to maximize the impact and effectiveness of your actions.

In all things, timing is paramount and doing the right thing at the wrong time is equivalent to doing the wrong thing. Consequently, and paradoxically, for some situations, taking action means being patient and waiting for the right moment to produce the best possible result.

<u>3/ Then put yourself in an optimal state of physical and emotional energy.</u>

Don't forget that the quality of your actions will be -by far- more important than the quantity. Your physical and emotional state is crucial to the success of what you want to achieve, so put yourself in optimal conditions. If you decide to do so, you can change your state in an instant! The keys to this are:

- A focus on solutions > Think about your "Why".
- A constructive state of mind > Put on catchy music that makes your state of mind positive!
- Good hydration > Drink a very large glass of water.
- A series of deep breaths > Go outside and take a big breath of fresh air.
- A more energetic and reactive body > Do 10 minutes of trampoline or go jogging.
- Good nutrition > Get back in control of your diet by eliminating junk food and eating lots more green vegetables.

<u>4/ Take action by taking the first steps.</u> The first steps, no matter how small, set in motion a dynamic. It can be a simple phone call, an e-mail or even a search on the Internet, it doesn't matter, but take action right away!

Don't be impressed by a possible long way to go and keep in mind this wisdom of Lao Tzu: "A journey of 1,000 leagues always begins with a first step!"

<u>5/ Finally, regardless of the difficulties and the slaps you're bound to take, keep acting,</u> amplify the movement and start producing results.

What is the priority solution I am considering to solve my problem? (see previous step)

_____
_____
_____

What is the list of all the actions to be taken? Which ones are important? Which are urgent? Is it preferable to carry them out in a particular order? If so, which one? Why is this?

_____
_____
_____
_____
_____
_____
_____
_____
_____
_____
_____
_____
_____
_____
_____
_____

Is there a particular timing or agenda that I need to take into account in order to maximize my actions? If so, which one? Why?

_____
_____
_____
_____
_____
_____
_____
_____
_____
_____

What actions can I take to optimize my physical and emotional energy?

_____
_____
_____
_____
_____
_____
_____
_____
_____
_____

What are the first steps I will take <u>today</u> to get the momentum going?

_____
_____
_____
_____
_____
_____
_____
_____
_____
_____
_____
_____

What are the next actions and steps that will follow and that I can start anticipating now?

_____
_____
_____
_____
_____
_____

_____
_____
_____
_____
_____
_____
_____
_____
_____
_____
_____
_____

And now, action!

_____

> "Some people want it to happen, some wish it would happen, others make it happen."
>
> *Michael Jordan*

_____

Chapter 6

Step 6: Identify the results you have achieved and continually adjust your approach until you get the results you are looking for

Step 6: Identify the results you have achieved and continually adjust your approach until you get the results you are looking for

Imperatively, if you take action, you will get results. However, don't expect that all your actions will always bring you the results you hope for. Some will be successful. Others will bring you unexpected but very positive results. Others will give you more mixed results. And some of the actions you will take will, for many of them, even be a complete waste of time or cause you additional problems that you will also have to deal with. That's how it is, it's part of the process.

So, if certain results don't meet your expectations, don't be emotionally attached to them. Don't see them as failures, but rather as learning and signposts that will help you adjust your future actions.

At the end of the day, remember that you are in control of your life and that it is up to you to collect the gains and lessons learned from these initial results in order to, literally, effectively steer this 6th step of the problem solving process. And like everything else you steer, there is a balance to be found, specific to each situation. A subtle mix of art, science, experience and technique.

To help you successfully manage this crucial step, here is the thread that I invite you to follow:

- Observe and analyze the first results obtained.

- Learn the lessons from these results.

- Evolve in your approach by testing other things and/or testing the same things but in a different way.

- Adapt yourself to the different situations and challenges that arise.

- Value what works.

- Remains open and flexible.

- Amplifies the process by increasing both the quantity and quality of the actions carried out.

Remember, there is no such thing as failure, only results. Depending on what you learn from these first elements, keep a positive frame of mind and continue to act massively. Re-evaluate the new results by adjusting your approach until you get the results you want.

Also keep in mind that some problems are not solved overnight and that it is often essential to have a long-term vision. Don't forget your "Why" and stay focused and determined!

What actions have I taken?
_____
_____
_____
_____
_____
_____
_____

What were the first results?

What is positive about these results? What new elements do they bring? Do they bring me closer to the solution? What have I understood thanks to them?

_____
_____
_____
_____
_____
_____
_____
_____
_____
_____
_____

How can I evolve in my approach by testing other things and/or testing the same things but in a different way?

_____
_____
_____
_____
_____
_____
_____
_____

As a result of these actions, what new challenges do I face? What do I need to do to manage them effectively?

_____
_____
_____
_____
_____
_____
_____
_____
_____
_____
_____
_____
_____

How can I enhance what works to further optimize results?

_____
_____
_____
_____
_____
_____

What do I learn from these situations and how can I use what I learn to get even closer to solving my problem?

What are the next actions I will take?

In order to obtain even more and better results, how can I increase the quantity but also -and above all- the quality of the actions I undertake?

_____
_____
_____
_____
_____
_____
_____
_____
_____
_____
_____
_____

IMPORTANT: You must now **repeat step 6** as many times as necessary until your problem is solved.

_____

"There is only one way to fail, and that is to give up before you've succeeded!"

Olivier Lockert

Chapter 7

Step 7: Welcome your successes but also accept what cannot be changed by using the emotion generated as a leverage for your life

Step 7: Welcome your successes but also accept what cannot be changed by using the emotion generated as a leverage for your life

We are coming to the end of our conversation and first of all I would like to congratulate you for following this problem solving process to the end. I hope this process has been helpful to you in some way. If it has, don't hesitate to spread the word around you and put a positive spin on online bookshops such as cultura.fr, fnac.com or Amazon.fr (In addition to helping future readers make their choice, the comments excite the algorithms of the platforms which, in turn, give the book better visibility). Also, if you have any questions, remarks or comments to make, don't hesitate to take a few minutes to send me a message directly:

www.geraldvignaud.com/livre-contact

However, before leaving us, I would like to talk to you in this last stage about some problems, some situations that sometimes occur in life and which are as painful as they are insoluble. I am thinking, for example, of things such as the love of one's life being irreversibly taken away, the loss of the use of one's legs, or the death of a loved one who is very dear to us.

I deeply believe that for every problem there is a solution. But I also believe that sometimes this solution is to accept the fact that there is no solution and that we must therefore learn to live with a given situation. In life, nobody avoids pain; and when it happens to you, you have two options: either you endure it or you transform it. Each ordeal, each suffering can also bring something wonderful. This is why in life it is often the most positive people who have encountered the most problems and suffered the most.

This is obviously not the easiest thing to do, but when you are faced with a painful and insoluble situation, the solution is to decide to accept it. Learn to let go and use the powerful emotion generated as a leverage for your life.

---

*"Sometimes man may be required
simply to accept fate, to bear his cross."*

Viktor Frankl

And it's about the last thing I'd like to talk to you about now. If the problem you are experiencing today falls into the "insoluble" category, make sure that its consequence is constructive for you by transforming the pain you feel into a powerful leverage that will give you the strength to take your life and your contribution to the world to a higher level.

To conclude, I would like to share with you this quotation from Albert Einstein with which I personally agree 100% and on which I leave you to meditate: "No problem can be solved from the same level of consciousness that created it."

And what if this was the ultimate goal of life:

Reaching higher levels of consciousness?

About the author

Gérald Vignaud is a graduate of the Business Mastery and the prestigious Mastery University. He has had an exceptional career in network marketing, becoming *Senior Vice President of* one of the most important companies in the industry. As a recognized expert in the industry, Gérald has trained and coached tens of thousands of people.

As a personal development coach, he has always taught that the key to success and, more importantly, to personal fulfilment lies in accepting oneself by assuming and working on one's difference, one's X-factor.

An expert in personal transformation, his first client was himself. An addict for almost 10 years, Gérald was able to make decisions and take action. He has implemented the strategies he now teaches to get off drugs and propel his life towards exceptional personal and professional success.

For several years, he has inspired, advised and worked with many people from all social/professional categories, including self-employed people, business leaders, top athletes, politicians and celebrities.

As a business consultant, Gérald understands and possesses the keys and strategies to help companies in all sectors reinvent themselves. He helps them re-energize themselves to redirect them towards the more positive and stable results they desire.

A **renowned speaker,** Gérald regularly appears before audiences ranging from 100 to 15,000 people and has shared the stage with personalities such as Chris Widener, **Darren Hardy and** Donald J. Trump.

An interviewer and passionate traveller, Gérald has listened to and learned from the thousands of people he has met over the course of his life.

An iconoclastic entrepreneur, Gérald is the founder and CEO of **different.land,** a personal development platform unique in the world. It focuses on the idea that the three major keys to creating a better future are education, ecology and healthy technology, and that all three are interconnected. The different.land website aims to help educate, inspire and nurture a new generation of leaders. One that will be responsible for building a much-needed better world for tomorrow, one that we will leave to our children.

A true nature lover, Gérald is notably the co-founder of the association SOS Océan. In partnership with the association Soupe de plastique, its mission is to inform, to make people understand the challenges that threaten our seas and oceans and to act to try to preserve them. More generally, Gérald also campaigns for better resource management and greater respect for our planet's ecosystems.

A true "Learning Junkie", Gérald constantly seeks to learn, to reinvent himself and to set the bar higher and higher in his life.

Gérald's mission is to help build present and future generations by helping people develop their differences and multiply their personal, professional and financial values.

If you would like Gérald Vignaud to speak at your event,
please contact us directly via the website:

www.geraldvignaud.com

"If a problem is fixable, if a situation is such that you can do something about it, then there is no need to worry. If it's not fixable, then there is no help in worrying. There is no benefit in worrying whatsoever."

The Dalaï Lama